MW01601459

THE BEAST WITHIN
A Journey from Separation to Wholeness
by
Giorgi Khatiashvili

First Edition 2026
ISBN: 9798261758914
Design and layout by Giorgi Khatiashvili

# Preface

The Beast, the Mirror, and the Work of Wholeness

This book was born from my own analysis, years of sitting on both sides of the couch and from the long process of writing my master's thesis, where theory first began to turn into lived experience.

It was also born from listening: listening to patients as they searched for words that could hold their pain; listening to myths and dreams that spoke in symbols long before language; and listening to that quiet inner voice that insists on truth even when it trembles.

Again and again, I found the same pattern: a wound at the beginning, a mask built to survive, and a secret longing to return to what is real.

In psychoanalytic language, we call it separation trauma or the formation of the false self. In spiritual language, it is the exile from paradise. In the language of fairy tales, it is the moment when Beauty first meets the Beast. However we name it, the story is universal.

I wrote these pages to make that story visible again not as theory but as lived truth. I wanted to speak to both the analyst and the artist, the parent and the seeker, anyone who has ever felt torn between wildness and goodness, freedom and belonging. The aim is not to add another self-help method to the world but to offer a mirror in which the reader may recognize their own aliveness.

The journey that follows moves from psychology to mythology, from the nursery to the classroom, from the personal to the collective. It draws on Winnicott's understanding of the true self, Alice Miller's critique of poisonous pedagogy, Rudolf

Steiner's vision of spiritual education, and the timeless wisdom carried in stories and symbols.

If there is a single message beneath it all, it is this: We do not need to kill the Beast to become human. We need to look into its eyes until we remember that it is us.

This book is written with gratitude to the teachers seen and unseen who showed me that self-understanding can be an art and that art can be a path to knowing oneself. May it serve anyone who wishes to live more truthfully, love more deeply, and bring a little more aliveness into the world.

Giorgi Khatiashvili

# Introduction

## The First Wound and the Hidden Map

Every human life begins with a rupture.
We arrive as one body divided: inside becomes outside, warmth becomes air, unity becomes distance.
The shock of that separation leaves an imprint that never fully fades.
From it arise our longings for safety, recognition, and love.

Most of life is spent trying to heal that first wound.
We seek mirrors that will tell us we exist—parents, partners, teachers, audiences, gods.
When those mirrors fail, we build substitutes: roles, achievements, and images.
These protect us, but they also harden us.
The self that was born to breathe begins to perform.

Yet beneath every mask, the original creature still stirs—the vital, sensing, instinctual self I call **the Beast**.
It is neither good nor bad; it simply wants to live.
The tragedy of modern life is that we are taught to fear it, to trade vitality for approval.
Out of that fear we create the **Monster**—the False Self that functions smoothly while feeling hollow.

This book traces the journey of reconciliation between those two parts.
It follows a map older than psychology: the symbolic language of myth and fairy tale.
In those stories we find our psychic anatomy drawn in images—the rose of longing, the mirror of self-recognition, the dragon of life force, the ring of relationship.
They are not fantasies but blueprints of transformation.

The chapters that follow move in four arcs:

1. **The First Wound** — how birth and separation awaken the Beast and the need for mirroring.
2. **The Mirror of Stories** — how myths like *Beauty and the Beast* reveal our inner dramas and offer paths of healing.
3. **The Making of the Monster** — how culture and education train us to distrust instinct and worship performance.
4. **The Return to Wholeness** — how to live with the Beast consciously through creativity, love, and a new pedagogy of aliveness.

Each section blends analytic understanding with symbolic imagination and practical reflection.
The intention is not to instruct but to invite—to help the reader feel seen, thought with, and accompanied on their own journey toward authenticity.

You may read these chapters as essays, meditations, or mirrors.
Their language moves between the head and the heart, between analysis and poetry.
Some passages will feel theoretical, others deeply personal; together they form a single movement—from exile to homecoming.

Read slowly, letting the ideas breathe.
Then you may begin to sense the same rhythm that guides the psyche itself: expansion and contraction, longing and rest, loss and return.
That rhythm is life teaching us how to heal.
It is the heartbeat of the Beast inside us, waiting not for control but for contact.

Welcome to the journey.

ॐ

## Chapter One

### The First Wound: When We Fall Out of Eden

We begin our human story not in sin, but in separation.
A moment comes when the world that has always been *us*
suddenly becomes *outside* of us.
Warmth turns to air.  The heartbeat we knew as rhythm
becomes silence.
What had no boundary now has skin.
The paradise of fusion ends—not because we did something
wrong, but because life insists on birth.

Every human being carries the echo of that first rupture.
Otto Rank called it *the trauma of birth*: the primal shock of being
torn from unity into solitude.
Others, like Bowlby, framed it as the beginning of attachment—
a bridge built toward the one who now stands apart.
Whatever the language, the experience is the same: a fall from
Eden, a thunderclap of loss and longing.

### The Beast Is Born

Out of that shock rises what I call **the Beast.**

Not the monster of fairy tales or religion, but a creature of need—a body alive with hunger, sound, and movement.
It is the purest form of vitality we will ever know: the cry that summons the world, the grasping hand that says *I am here.*

The Beast is innocence with appetite.
It is our first self, unashamed and unrefined, driven by the simplest command—*connect with life.*
In those first hours, the newborn's cry is not rage or rebellion; it is the sound of the self declaring existence.

Rank wrote that civilization begins when we try to master this terror of separation.
Every culture, in its myths and rituals, carries a story of the expelled child—the journey from oneness to exile.
In Genesis, Adam and Eve leave the garden.
In Greek myth, Persephone descends into darkness.
In every cradle, an infant leaves the sea of the womb and enters the dry land of air.
And with that entrance, the Beast opens its eyes.

The Mother's Mirror

Donald Winnicott, the English pediatrician-analyst, said that when an infant looks at the mother's face, what it sees there is itself.
The gaze of the other becomes a mirror in which the self first appears.
"When I look," he wrote, "I am seen, therefore I exist."

If the mother's eyes are warm, responsive, alive, the baby meets its own aliveness mirrored back.
Joy moves in circles—smile to smile, breath to breath.

This is the birth of what Winnicott called the **True Self**—the spontaneous core that feels real because it has been recognized.

Daniel Stern later described this as *attunement*: the dance of small gestures through which caregiver and infant share a rhythm.
A touch, a tone, a look that says, *I feel you feeling me.*
In such moments, the infant's raw Beastness becomes safe enough to remain open.
The body relaxes; experience begins to organize itself; the world seems trustworthy.

When the Mirror Fails

But what if the mirror does not reflect?
If the face that greets the infant is empty, anxious, distracted— or demanding rather than receptive—the circle breaks.
The cry meets no echo.
The gaze meets no gaze.
The infant feels not seen but *dropped.*

Didier Anzieu, in *The Skin-Ego,* suggested that the psyche forms like a second skin.
When that envelope is punctured by absence or intrusion, the self feels flayed.
In daily life we sense this as *emptiness*—a word adults use for what began as simple terror.
Something inside whispers, *I'm not safe; I might disappear.*

To survive that feeling, the child begins to build armor.
Winnicott named this armor the **False Self**—a set of behaviors designed to preserve connection at any cost.

The smile that hides fear, the compliance that trades authenticity for approval, the early competence that wins love through performance.
Each layer says: *If I'm good enough, maybe I won't be left again.*

Alice Miller later called this *poisonous pedagogy*—the social training that rewards obedience and punishes spontaneity.
A child learns to read the emotional weather of the adults and adjust accordingly.
The Beast—once a pure expression of being—is gradually tamed into a socially acceptable creature.
The energy that was meant for growth is rerouted toward survival.

The Monster of Adaptation

Over years, this adaptation solidifies.
The armor becomes identity.
We say, "I'm the reliable one," or "I never make trouble," or "I always know what to do."
Underneath, the Beast still breathes, but quietly, waiting for warmth that will allow it to emerge.

This is what I call **the Monster**—not evil, but mechanical: the False Self that performs life instead of living it.
It smiles when sad, achieves when exhausted, helps when it needs help.
It may look admirable, yet it feels hollow.
The Monster's purpose is safety, not joy.
It would rather be loved for what it does than risk being rejected for what it is.

Winnicott saw this clearly in his patients who felt unreal despite success.

"Only when I am alone," one said, "do I feel alive."
The armor protects but isolates.
The more polished the performance, the deeper the hunger for recognition.

## Anxiety as Memory

John Bowlby, studying attachment, observed that infants separated from caregivers move through three predictable phases: protest, despair, and detachment.
Even as adults, we repeat these cycles—angry at absence, numb in loss, resigned to distance.
Each episode of anxiety, each moment of jealousy or panic, is an echo of that first protest: *Don't leave me.*

We rarely remember it consciously, yet our bodies do.
The rapid heartbeat, the tightening chest, the sudden sense of falling—these are not random.
They are the language of the Beast, remembering separation.
In therapy rooms across the world, people speak of emptiness, abandonment, burnout.
Beneath each story lies that early alarm.

Wilfred Bion described the caregiver as a *container* for the infant's unbearable feelings.
When the mother can "digest" the child's distress and return it in calm form, the child learns that emotions are survivable.
When she cannot, terror remains unprocessed; it floats in the psyche like undigested food.
Many of us, decades later, still carry that residue.
We call it anxiety, but it is really undigested experience.

## The Beast Never Dies

And yet—the miracle—is that the Beast survives.
It hides beneath the layers of compliance and competence, waiting for permission to breathe again.
You can feel it stir in moments of awe: when music moves you to tears, when you fall in love, when creation pours through your hands.
In those instants, the armor loosens and something ancient looks out through your eyes.

The task of adulthood is not to slay this creature but to **befriend** it.
Every myth that warns us against the Beast also hides a secret promise: that what appears frightening may be the gateway to wholeness.
Beauty does not kill the Beast—she sees him.
Saint George's dragon can be read not as an enemy but as life-force misjudged.
The problem was never the Beast itself, but our inability to meet its hunger with compassion.

Rainer Maria Rilke wrote that perhaps all the dragons in our lives are "princesses waiting to see us act, just once, with beauty and courage."
What we call our demons are often unloved forms of vitality.
When they are seen, they transform.

Reflection for the Reader

Take a few quiet minutes.  Sit where you can breathe easily.  Let your attention rest on your body.
Notice sensations of warmth, pressure, or emptiness.
Then gently ask:

*What did I learn, very early, about showing my needs?*

*What did I have to do to keep love close?*
*Where in my life do I still hide the Beast to feel safe?*

Write a few sentences without censoring.
The goal is not analysis but remembering—the felt sense of how you learned to exist.
Often the first word that arises ("quiet," "good," "strong," "invisible") names the armor.
Beneath it lies the creature that still wants to breathe.

When you can meet that creature with curiosity instead of judgment, the first wound begins to heal.
The fall from Eden becomes not a curse but a passage—the necessary distance from which love can be seen, chosen, and shared.

ṭ

## Chapter Two

Why Stories Know Us: The Mirror of Fairy Tales

There is a moment in every childhood when the world of fairy tales feels more real than the world of adults.
The storybook opens, the voice begins, and the ordinary room dissolves.
A forest appears, a castle gleams in the distance, a creature breathes in the dark.
The child does not question whether the tale is true; the body already knows it is.

What the child recognizes, long before language can explain it, is the **logic of the soul.**
Fairy tales speak in images that predate thought—hunger, loss, love, fear, transformation.
They are not about dragons or witches but about the parts of us that must be faced, integrated, or redeemed.
As Marie-Louise von Franz wrote, "Fairy tales are the purest and simplest expression of collective unconscious psychic processes."

We may forget the details of childhood stories, but the feeling they left behind remains: the tremor when the Beast first

appears, the relief when Beauty returns, the satisfaction when love turns curse into blessing.
These sensations are the psyche's earliest lessons in emotional truth.

## The Story as Mirror

In the last chapter, we explored how the infant first finds itself in the mother's eyes.
A fairy tale performs a similar function for the developing mind—it **mirrors inner experience** at a symbolic distance.
When a child listens to "Beauty and the Beast," it is not learning about some external moral code; it is watching its own inner life play out safely on the stage of imagination.

Bruno Bettelheim, in *The Uses of Enchantment*, wrote that fairy tales give the child "a frame within which he can master the internal conflicts that disturb him."
By projecting fear, anger, and desire onto characters, the child begins to see feelings as survivable.
The wolf, the witch, the stepmother, the Beast—all these figures carry emotional weight so the child doesn't have to bear it alone.

In this way, stories are **containers**, much like Bion's concept of the caregiver who holds unbearable feelings until they can be understood.
The tale listens for us, digests the chaos of emotion, and returns it as pattern, rhythm, meaning.

## The Language of Symbols

Unlike modern entertainment, fairy tales rarely describe thoughts or motives.

They speak in **symbols**, a language that reaches deeper than logic.
A forest is never just a forest—it is the unknown within.
A rose is not a flower but the heart's longing for beauty and connection.
A ring is not jewelry but the circle of relationship, the eternal return of love.

These symbols operate below awareness, like dreams.
Carl Jung saw them as expressions of the *collective unconscious*: the shared storehouse of human experience.
Through them, we inherit ancient wisdom without needing to explain it.
The stories that survive are those whose symbols still match the structure of the psyche.

This is why, across cultures, we find the same motifs repeating— the lost child, the forbidden room, the talking animal, the magical helper.
They are not coincidences but reflections of universal psychological tasks: separation, temptation, reconciliation, individuation.

## Beauty and the Beast: A Tale of Inner Relationship

Among all fairy tales, few mirror the human condition as powerfully as **"Beauty and the Beast."**
It begins, as many tales do, with loss: a merchant's fortune ruined, his family exiled to the countryside.
When the father attempts to return home, he plucks a rose for his beloved daughter—an innocent gesture that awakens the Beast's wrath.
The father must choose between his own life and his daughter's freedom.

Beauty volunteers to go in his place.

Already the story contains the themes of the first wound: separation, sacrifice, and the awakening of need.
The Beast, hidden in his castle, represents the raw instinctual life that society fears—the same vitality we called the *Beast* in the previous chapter.
He lives outside the village, beyond the boundaries of propriety, surrounded by enchantment and loneliness.

When Beauty meets him, she experiences fear and pity in equal measure.
The Beast does not harm her; instead, he asks the same question every evening: *"Will you marry me?"*
Night after night she refuses, yet gradually her compassion grows.
She begins to see the creature's pain behind his appearance.
The turning point comes when she leaves him to visit her family and returns too late—the Beast is dying of grief.
Her tears and her confession of love break the spell.
The Beast transforms into a prince.

On the surface, the story reads as romantic redemption, but its psychological meaning is deeper.
Beauty represents the conscious, civilizing aspect of the self— the capacity to see, feel, and relate.
The Beast embodies the instinctual, passionate, animal part of being.
Their union symbolizes integration: the reconciliation of spirit and flesh, reason and desire, consciousness and instinct.

The Rose, the Mirror, and the Ring

Each symbol in the tale mirrors a developmental truth.

**The rose** is the symbol of longing—the pure request of the heart.
When the father plucks it, he repeats the primal act of separation: taking beauty from its source.
The Beast's rage is the rage of the wounded instinct whose connection has been stolen.
The rose also represents the need for love that persists despite danger—the same hunger that drives the newborn's first cry.

**The mirror**, often a gift within the tale, allows Beauty to see what happens beyond the castle.
Psychologically, it is the capacity for self-reflection—the function once provided by the mother's gaze.
When we internalize that mirror, we develop what Winnicott called the *capacity to be alone in the presence of another*: the ability to see ourselves without losing ourselves.

**The ring** symbolizes the cycle of relationship and return.
When Beauty uses it to travel between the castle and her family, it represents the balance between autonomy and attachment.
Mature love, the story suggests, is not fusion but rhythm—the freedom to leave and the faith to return.

Through these symbols, "Beauty and the Beast" teaches what Winnicott taught in analytic language: that love is not the absence of separation but the capacity to endure it without destroying either self or other.

When Culture Tames the Beast

Societies often reinterpret this story to reinforce social obedience—emphasizing Beauty's duty or patience rather than her perception and courage.

Yet the deeper message is not submission but **seeing**.
Beauty's act of love is not blind acceptance but genuine recognition.
She does not rescue the Beast by obeying him; she rescues him by understanding him.

In that sense, Beauty performs what every parent, therapist, or partner must eventually learn: to look at the other's Beast without fear, to mirror vitality instead of controlling it.
The healing power of the story lies in its model of *compassionate seeing*—what the psychoanalyst Heinz Kohut called *empathic attunement*, the bridge through which the self feels real.

## Why We Still Need Fairy Tales

Modern adults often dismiss fairy tales as naive, yet our cinemas and streaming services are filled with their descendants—superhero sagas, fantasy epics, love stories between flawed humans and mysterious forces.
We still need these mirrors.
Beneath our sophistication, the same child listens, waiting to see its inner life reflected.

When a story captures us, our nervous system recognizes pattern.
The heart quickens not because the plot is exciting but because the psyche is being named.
We feel less alone.
The Beast inside us hears its own story and softens.

In therapy, I often invite people to recall the tale that most haunted them in childhood.
Without fail, it corresponds to their central psychological theme.

The client who loved *Cinderella* often struggles with invisibility and recognition.

The one who feared *Hansel and Gretel* wrestles with abandonment.

The one who adored *Beauty and the Beast* seeks to reconcile instinct and tenderness.

Fairy tales are maps of the soul drawn in the ink of imagination.

## The Inner Marriage

Ultimately, "Beauty and the Beast" ends not with conquest but with marriage.

This union is not only romantic; it is **psychic integration**—the conscious self embracing the instinctual self.

In Jungian terms, Beauty meets her *shadow* and discovers wholeness.

The prince who emerges is not a different being but the same energy now seen through love.

Every healing process follows this pattern.

The feelings we once feared—anger, desire, sadness—become transformed when recognized.

The Beast becomes articulate.

The self expands to include what was rejected.

As the alchemists said, *"What was once poison becomes medicine."*

## Reflection for the Reader

Take a few minutes to recall a story that has stayed with you since childhood.

Write down the key images that arise—the setting, the characters, the turning point.

Then ask:

*What part of me is still living this story?*
*Which character do I most resist or pity?*
*What would transformation look like here, if love were possible?*

You may discover that your favorite tale was never about someone else.
It was your own inner life speaking in symbols, waiting to be heard.

ቶ

# Chapter Three

## Beast vs. Monster: When Culture Trains Our Instincts

The Beast we met in the beginning was innocent.
It wanted only to live, to reach, to breathe.
But from the first moment it appeared in the world, it met resistance.
Parents, teachers, priests, governments—each in their own way—whispered the same warning:
*Control yourself.*

From that whisper, civilization begins.
It teaches us to trade instinct for conformity, spontaneity for safety, aliveness for approval.
The transformation is so gradual that we rarely notice it.
We call it education, etiquette, success.
But underneath, something wild and luminous begins to dim.

## The Birth of the Monster

When the Beast's vitality is judged or shamed, it retreats underground.
In its place, we build an efficient substitute: the **Monster.**
Unlike the Beast, the Monster is not instinctual but strategic.

It learns to read the room, to anticipate expectations, to hide hunger behind performance.
It becomes the perfect citizen, the model student, the reliable friend.
It keeps us alive—but not alive enough.

Winnicott called this the **False Self**: a protective structure that emerges when the environment demands adaptation before authenticity.
He wrote that the False Self "develops out of compliance," while the True Self "can only emerge in a state of freedom."
For the infant, freedom means the ability to express without fear of abandonment.
For the adult, it means the ability to live without apology.

The tragedy is that the world rewards the Monster.
It promotes the efficient over the authentic, the obedient over the original.
Children learn early that love is conditional—based on achievement, politeness, and control.
By adolescence, the Monster speaks fluently:
"Don't be too much."
"Don't fail."
"Don't need."

The voice sounds like reason, but it is really fear in a civilized costume.

The Good Child and the Quiet Soul

Alice Miller described how many gifted, sensitive children become "good children" to protect fragile parents.
They sense, without words, that their authenticity might overwhelm the adult.

So they learn to soothe, to please, to perform.
They become experts in empathy at the cost of their own feeling.

Such children grow into adults who are competent but empty.
They manage crises, organize families, and succeed professionally, yet often confess, "I don't know what I feel."
Their energy, once wild and creative, has been harnessed into survival mode.

This loss of vitality is not a moral failure—it is an adaptation to love's conditions.
The psyche sacrifices spontaneity to preserve attachment.
The Monster, for all its artificiality, is a child's act of devotion.

Culture as Training Ground

The Monster is not created only by families; it is reinforced by culture.
Schools reward correct answers more than curiosity.
Corporations prize productivity over imagination.
Religions, in their distorted forms, punish desire rather than illuminate it.
The collective message is clear: *Do not trust your inner fire.*

Michel Foucault observed that modern society no longer needs prisons to enforce obedience; we internalize surveillance.
We watch ourselves.
We become both prisoner and guard.
Social media has turned this into ritual—performing a version of ourselves we hope will be loved.
We trade authenticity for attention, forgetting that the heart cannot be fooled by likes.

Culture's genius is its ability to convince the captive that the cage is comfort.
We call exhaustion "hard work," anxiety "ambition," numbness "maturity."
The Monster thrives under these names, polite and tireless.

## The Cost of Control

But control has a cost.
What is repressed does not disappear; it waits.
The Beast, denied expression, returns through the body—panic attacks, insomnia, addiction, depression.
Symptoms are the Beast's messages delivered in disguise.
They say, *I am still here. I will not vanish.*

Wilfred Bion suggested that when emotion cannot be thought, it becomes acted or somatized.
That is why therapy often begins where words fail.
The task is not to destroy the Monster but to translate the Beast's language into human speech again.

When a person in therapy says, "I feel nothing," what they often mean is, "I once felt everything, and it was too much."
The Monster learned to mute the radio to survive the noise.
Healing begins when we dare to raise the volume slightly—to let life's sound return.

## When Goodness Becomes Violence

There is a quiet kind of violence in perfection.
People who never shout, never break, never rest often carry unbearable tension.
They harm themselves gently—with overwork, self-criticism, chronic caretaking.

This is the Monster's morality: goodness used as armor.

Culture celebrates this violence.
We praise those who sacrifice sleep for success, who smile through pain, who "keep it together."
But what if holding it together is what breaks us?

Alice Miller warned that a society built on obedience produces emotional blindness.
When feelings are disciplined out of existence, compassion erodes.
We no longer recognize suffering—our own or others'.
The Monster becomes collective; institutions act without empathy.
The Beast, banished, returns as war, exploitation, environmental destruction—the body of the world screaming where individuals could not.

Remembering the Body

To reclaim the Beast, we must begin with the body—the place where it still lives.
Breathe deeply, and the Monster grows nervous.
Move freely, and the old instincts wake.
The body is honest; it tells us what the mind denies.

Alexander Lowen, founder of bioenergetic analysis, believed that emotional health is measured by the body's capacity for pleasure and expression.
He wrote, "The more alive the body, the more real the self."
Our culture, obsessed with image, reverses this: we sculpt the body instead of feeling it.
We turn flesh into display rather than experience.

To feel is to risk vulnerability, but it is also to reclaim power.
When we inhabit the body, the Beast no longer needs to shout through symptoms.
It can speak softly, as pulse, rhythm, desire.

## The Gentle Revolt

To live authentically in an inauthentic culture is an act of quiet rebellion.
The task is not to destroy civilization but to humanize it—to bring soul back into structure.
This begins with small refusals: the pause before automatic yes, the breath before apology, the choice to rest when the world demands performance.

Each act of honesty weakens the Monster's rule.
Each moment of self-kindness feeds the Beast instead of the armor.
Over time, vitality returns—not as chaos but as presence.

The poet Mary Oliver asked, "Tell me, what is it you plan to do with your one wild and precious life?"
The answer cannot come from the Monster; it can only come from the Beast, the part that still feels wonder.

## Reflection for the Reader

Pause for a moment and ask yourself:

*What parts of me were praised for being "good" rather than being real?*
*Where does my energy go—to living or to maintaining control?*
*What would happen if I let one small impulse of the Beast be expressed today?*

Write down whatever comes.
Then, do one simple act that honors it: stretch, rest, speak a truth, make something beautiful.
You may discover that goodness and aliveness are not enemies after all.

## Chapter Four

### Don't Kill the Dragon: Relating to the Beast with Skill

We have been taught to fear our own fire.
From childhood fairy tales to modern education, the message repeats: *Be good. Be calm. Tame the wild thing inside you.*
Yet every myth that warns us to slay the dragon hides another truth—
that the dragon guards treasure,
and whoever kills it too quickly loses the gift it was meant to protect.

The **Beast** we met in birth and the **Monster** we built to survive are not enemies.
They are two poles of the same energy: instinct and adaptation, vitality and control.
The task of maturity is not to destroy one for the other but to hold them in creative tension.
True mastery is not domination; it is relationship.

### The Dragon as Life Force

Across cultures, dragons embody the elemental powers of nature: fire, air, water, earth intertwined.
In Western legend, Saint George slays the dragon to rescue the maiden.

In Eastern traditions, dragons bring wisdom, rain, and renewal.
The difference reveals a cultural split: where the West sees
danger, the East sees energy.

Psychologically, the dragon represents the **instinctual life
force**—raw libido, creative fire, the unconscious pulse that
animates everything.
Freud called it *Eros.* Jung called it *the Self's energy seeking
consciousness.*
It can burn or illuminate depending on how we meet it.

When we repress this energy, it turns against us as anxiety,
addiction, or aggression.
When we express it blindly, it consumes us.
The art is to befriend it—to let the fire warm without scorching,
to ride the dragon instead of killing it.

Why We Fear Our Own Fire

Civilization is built on the attempt to manage instinct.
Laws, religion, and education arise from our need to feel safe
within our own power.
But in protecting ourselves from chaos, we have exiled vitality
itself.
Modern people often feel lifeless not because life is absent, but
because it is overcontrolled.

Winnicott noted that when spontaneity is crushed early, the
individual becomes compliant but unreal.
The same pattern repeats collectively: societies that fear passion
become rigid, bureaucratic, subtly violent.
Repressed fire finds expression through war, exploitation, or
obsession—destruction disguised as order.

Our fear of the Beast, then, is really fear of our own **aliveness.**
To feel fully means to risk change, loss, desire.
The Monster promises safety through numbness.
But the price of numbness is meaning.

## Relating, Not Resisting

To relate to the Beast skillfully, we must replace the language of
*control* with the language of *relationship.*
Imagine standing before a wild horse.
You cannot beat it into obedience.
You approach with presence, tone, and rhythm until trust grows.
The same applies inwardly: emotions respond to attention, not
punishment.

When anger arises, the goal is not to suppress it but to listen.
What boundary was crossed? What desire ignored?
Feelings are messages, not moral failures.
Violence occurs only when we silence the messenger.

Bion called growth "learning from experience."
Even painful feelings contain data.
When the mind can hold them, they transform into insight.
The dragon's fire becomes light.

## Containment, Not Repression

Containment is not the same as control.
It means *holding energy with awareness.*
A clay pot does not deny the water inside—it gives it shape.

In daily life, containment looks like pausing before reacting,
breathing through impulse, naming what arises.

This creates a space between stimulus and response where consciousness can act.
Viktor Frankl wrote, "Between stimulus and response there is a space. In that space lies our power to choose our response. In our response lies our growth and our freedom."

That space is the hearth where the dragon becomes ally.

In therapy, containment happens through relationship.
The analyst's calm presence allows the client to feel emotions too intense to manage alone.
Gradually, the capacity for containment becomes internalized—the person learns to hold their own fire.

## From Discipline to Dialogue

Most traditions confuse discipline with suppression.
True discipline comes from *discere*—to learn.
It is not control from outside but awareness from within.
A musician practices scales not to silence creativity but to express it clearly.
Likewise, inner discipline gives form to energy without diminishing it.

The Zen master said, "The tighter you hold the bow, the less the arrow flies."
Restraint and release must alternate.
To live skillfully with the Beast, one must allow both passion and pause, both power and tenderness.

## Creativity as Alchemy

Art is one of the safest and most sacred ways to converse with the Beast.

When we paint, dance, write, or play music, the unconscious is given a voice.
Emotion turns to symbol; chaos to pattern.
The energy that could destroy becomes creation.

Jung's *Red Book* was such a dialogue—visions through which he met the figures of his psyche.
He warned that when the creative process is denied, neurosis appears.
"The artist," he said, "is the vehicle through which the collective unconscious speaks."
But everyone carries that artist inside—the capacity to translate energy into meaning.

## The Alchemy of Relationship

No field tests our ability to hold the dragon's fire like relationship.
Love awakens the same forces that once birthed trauma—desire, dependency, fear of loss.
We project our Beast onto the other and then try to tame it in them.
Conflict follows not from incompatibility but from intensity.

When two people learn to witness each other's fire without judgment, intimacy deepens.
Instead of asking, "How do I stop you from hurting me?" they ask, "What is this energy teaching us?"
Then love becomes laboratory—each partner refining the other's ability to hold life.

The alchemists called this *coniunctio*—the sacred marriage of opposites.

It occurs whenever consciousness and instinct meet without domination.
The gold produced is not perfection but wholeness.

## Modern Dragons

Today our dragons wear new masks: ambition, technology, sexuality, competition.
The same energy that once fueled artists and explorers now powers markets and machines.
We cannot escape it; we can only choose how to relate.

Unacknowledged, it burns as greed and exploitation.
Acknowledged, it powers creativity, empathy, innovation.
The question for our era is no longer whether to slay the dragon but whether we can **ride it together**—to use its energy for connection rather than control.

## The Courage to Feel

All this requires courage—the courage to feel fully without running away.
Rilke advised, "Let everything happen to you: beauty and terror. Just keep going. No feeling is final."
To live that way is to reclaim the full spectrum of being.

Fear, anger, lust, envy—all contain information.
When we stop moralizing emotions and start listening to them, we find that beneath every "negative" feeling lies a positive intention.
Anger protects boundaries; fear preserves life; desire seeks union.
Recognizing this turns battle into dialogue.

## Children and the Untamed Heart

Children naturally know this until taught otherwise.
They rage, cry, laugh, and then return to play.
Their feelings move like weather—intense but impermanent.
They do not fear their own fire.

Our task is not to suppress that fire but to model **regulated vitality**—how to stay connected while feeling deeply.
A parent who says, "I'm angry, and I still love you," gives the greatest lesson of all: that emotion and relationship can coexist.

## The Spiritual Dimension

Many spiritual paths aim for this same reconciliation.
In the East, the serpent *kundalini* represents energy rising through consciousness.
Christian mystics spoke of divine fire.
Taoist sages rode the dragon of *chi*.
All describe instinct ascending into awareness.

True spirituality does not flee the body; it includes it.
The Beast, when honored, becomes a gateway to transcendence.
Teilhard de Chardin wrote, "We are not human beings having a spiritual experience; we are spiritual beings having a human experience."
To kill the dragon would be to sever the bridge between heaven and earth.

## Integrating the Beast

Integration is a daily practice, not a single awakening.

Each time we pause instead of react, breathe instead of suppress, speak truth instead of perform, we reclaim a piece of the Beast.
Over time, the inner world shifts—from battlefield to dialogue.

In therapy, in art, in meditation, we meet the dragon repeatedly.
Sometimes as grief, sometimes as joy.
Each encounter refines us.
Eventually, the boundaries between Beast and Self blur—we realize they were never separate.
The energy we feared was always life reaching toward us.

## Reflection for the Reader

Find a quiet moment.
Bring to mind a feeling you usually avoid—anger, jealousy, lust, shame, anxiety.
Instead of analyzing it, notice where it lives in the body.
Breathe into it and ask:

*What are you protecting?*
*What do you need from me?*

Write down what comes, even if it makes no sense.
This is the beginning of dialogue with your dragon.
With practice, its answers become clearer, wiser, often kind.
You may find that beneath fear lies vitality longing to serve life.

## Closing

Early icons of Saint George show not a warrior killing a dragon but a man gazing into its eyes.
Between them is stillness—a recognition.

Later, the story changed to suit a culture that taught control through conquest.
But the truer image remains: George and the dragon, eye to eye.

To gaze without panic—that is mastery.
To meet the fire without extinguishing it—that is love.
Only then do we become whole: creatures of both light and flame, capable of holding the entirety of our nature with grace.

❦

## Chapter Five

### Home and Classroom: A New Pedagogy of Aliveness

Education begins long before a child enters school.
It begins the moment a cry meets an answering presence.
From that first exchange, the human being starts learning: *Is the world safe for my aliveness?*
Every later lesson—at home, in classrooms, in relationships—
echoes that first response.

For centuries, education has been designed to civilize the Beast:
to train instinct into discipline, curiosity into compliance.
It created functioning citizens but lonely souls.
A true education does not tame life; it teaches it to move gracefully.

### From Obedience to Awareness

Traditional schooling begins with control.
It assumes that the child is a raw material to be shaped.
But every child already carries an inner rhythm; the teacher's task is not to mold it, but to listen to it.

Donald Winnicott's idea of *"good-enough mothering"* applies to all education.
A good teacher, like a good parent, offers **reliable presence**—not perfection.
Mistakes are allowed; repair is possible.
Through this rhythm of rupture and restoration, trust grows, and trust becomes curiosity.

Alice Miller warned that obedience-based education teaches children to betray their own truth.
"When the price of love is self-betrayal," she wrote, "the child becomes intelligent but disconnected."
The new pedagogy reverses that contract: love must never depend on suppression.

The Atmosphere of the Soul

Children learn far more from emotional climate than from words.
The home or classroom acts like weather: if it is tense, learning contracts; if it is warm, curiosity unfolds.

Rudolf Steiner called this the *soul atmosphere*—the invisible tone that nourishes or stifles growth.
He insisted that rhythm, beauty, and imagination are the foundation of learning.
"The heart of the child," he said, "must be reached through beauty before the intellect awakens through truth."

When a child sings, paints, gardens, and dreams alongside reading and arithmetic, the Beast and the mind grow together.
Thinking and feeling become allies.

The Myth of Performance

Modern schooling equates worth with results—grades, prizes, test scores.
It mirrors the Monster's logic: *I must perform to belong.*
Under this weight, curiosity withers and anxiety blooms.

Carol Dweck's research on *mindset* confirms what psychoanalysts intuited:
Praise for performance breeds fear of failure; praise for effort and curiosity breeds resilience.
The difference is subtle but transformative.
A pedagogy of aliveness values **process over perfection.**
It asks, "What did you discover?" instead of "What did you achieve?"

## The Adult as Gardener

Adults imagine they build children like architects build houses.
But human growth follows seasons, not blueprints.
The adult's role is closer to that of a gardener: to create conditions where what already lives can unfold.

Gardening requires patience and trust.
You cannot pull a flower open.
You water, you wait, you watch the sun do its work.
Likewise, a child's unfolding Self needs space, rhythm, and protection—not premature evaluation.

Steiner called education *"an art of awakening what already lives within."*
Winnicott would have said the same: holding strong enough for safety, open enough for freedom.

## Boundaries that Breathe

A pedagogy of aliveness does not mean permissiveness.
Boundaries are the banks of the river; they give direction to flow.
A child without boundaries feels abandoned; a child with too many feels imprisoned.
Balance is achieved through relationship, not rules.

When an adult can say, "I see your anger, and I will help you stay safe with it,"
the child learns that feeling and connection can coexist.
This is emotional literacy: understanding that emotion is natural, behavior is guided, and relationship remains intact.

## The Power of Repair

Every conflict or misunderstanding is an opportunity for education.
When adults apologize, listen, and restore connection, children learn empathy through example.
A teacher who says, "I spoke sharply and I'm sorry," teaches more about courage than any textbook.
Repair turns authority from fear into trust.

## Restoring Play

Play is the native language of the Beast.
It is how the child experiments with power and possibility.
Modern life, obsessed with productivity, erodes this language.
Even leisure becomes scheduled, competitive, monetized.
The result is a generation who know how to win but not how to wonder.

Winnicott wrote that play is the space "where the self feels real."
In play, imagination and reality dance.
A child who builds a sandcastle learns creation and loss; a child who pretends learns empathy.
To restore play is to restore soul.

## The Teacher as Mirror

Children read faces more fluently than books.
They sense whether an adult is genuine or armored.
A teacher who is alive to their own feelings unconsciously gives permission for others to be alive.

Every educator must ask: *Which part of me teaches—the Beast or the Monster?*
When we teach from the Monster, we enforce order; when we teach from the Beast, we inspire curiosity.
Each classroom mirrors the inner world of its caretaker.

## Environment as Teacher

Light, colour, sound, and rhythm all educate.
Steiner called the environment "the third teacher."
A room with natural light and harmony teaches reverence better than moral lectures.
A day paced like breath—focus and rest, silence and song—calms the nervous system and deepens learning.
When rhythm is honoured, the Beast feels safe to participate.

## Re-Educating the Adult

The hardest part of creating a new pedagogy is re-educating the grown-ups.

Most of us were schooled through fear, comparison, or perfectionism.
We carry those scripts until we consciously rewrite them.

Forgiveness is the beginning.
Not to excuse what hurt us, but to stop repeating it.
Alice Miller called this becoming an *enlightened witness*—an adult who protects the next generation from what harmed their own.

## Toward a Culture of Aliveness

Imagine a society organized around the principle that every person has an inner rhythm, and education exists to bring it into harmony with the world.
Schools would resemble studios more than factories; homes would feel like gardens of experimentation.
Success would mean wholeness, not domination.

Such a culture would still have structure, but its discipline would arise from respect for life.
It would teach that the Beast is sacred energy—the dragon's fire that fuels creativity, empathy, and purpose.
It would raise citizens who know not only how to think, but how to feel.

## Reflection for the Reader

Take a moment to remember your own schooling.
Ask yourself:

*What kind of environment helped me grow—fear or curiosity?*
*Who allowed me to be fully alive?*
*Which parts of me went underground to survive?*

If you are a parent, teacher, or mentor, ask further:

*What atmosphere do I create?*
*Do I reward obedience or authenticity?*
*Do I model aliveness, or only speak of it?*

Then imagine one small change—a gesture, a tone, a moment of laughter—that could make your home or classroom a little more alive.

## Closing

The old pedagogy sought to tame life.
The new one seeks to collaborate with it.
Education at its highest level is not the transfer of information but the cultivation of soul—the art of awakening consciousness within the living stream of instinct.
When home and classroom become places where the Beast is welcomed and guided, civilization itself begins to heal.

The true goal of learning is not obedient adults but awakened humans: beings capable of thinking with their hearts and feeling with their minds.
In them, the dragon of vitality and the angel of awareness fly side by side.

ॐ

## Chapter Six

### Growing Wholeness: Daily Mirroring and Creative Practice

Healing is not a single revelation but a rhythm.
It unfolds like breath: expansion and rest, effort and release.
Each time we pause to feel, to notice, to stay, we grow another small cell of wholeness.
The Beast we feared becomes a companion; the Monster we built begins to sleep.
Life moves from performance to presence.

### The Need to Be Seen—Again and Again

Human beings never outgrow the need for mirroring.
As infants, we discover ourselves in another's eyes; as adults, we rediscover ourselves in empathy.
When someone looks at us with genuine attention, our inner world organizes.
When no one looks, we fragment.

But the miracle is that we can learn to offer that gaze to ourselves.
Self-mirroring is not vanity—it is care.
It means saying inwardly, *I see you. I hear you. You make sense.*
Over time, this inner witness becomes the quiet presence we once sought outside.

Rituals of Presence

Ritual gives rhythm to consciousness.
It need not be religious; any act done with intention becomes sacred.
Rituals mark the transition between sleep and waking, work and rest, isolation and contact.
They remind the Monster that structure can be gentle, and they tell the Beast that it is safe to return.

Try a few simple ones:

**The Morning Mirror** – Before the day begins, stand before your reflection.
Breathe.  Look into your own eyes as if greeting an old friend.
You may whisper, *Good morning, I'm here.*
It seems small, but it reestablishes connection between awareness and embodiment.

**The Evening Journal** – Each night, write a few sentences beginning with "Today I felt…"
Not what you did, but what you felt.
Even two honest lines restore continuity to the self.

**The Breath Pause** – Several times a day, stop and take three full breaths.
Feel the air move through the body that carries you.
This is Winnicott's "pause that allows aliveness."

**The Gratitude of Senses** – Choose one sensory experience each day—a colour, a scent, a texture—and attend to it completely.
Sensory attention is meditation in motion; it grounds the Beast in the present.

## Creativity as Dialogue

Creativity is not decoration—it is the psyche speaking.
Every time we make something—a meal, a melody, a thought—
we participate in the same process that shaped us.
Carl Jung wrote that "the creative act is the unconscious finding
expression."
When energy that was trapped in symptom finds form in art, it
becomes meaning.

You do not need talent, only sincerity.
When a child draws, they are not imitating; they are translating.
Adults can do the same.
Write without goal, paint without audience, move without
choreography.
Art heals not because it beautifies pain, but because it gives pain
a voice.

## The Body as Home

For centuries, spirituality has tried to transcend the body.
But the body is not an obstacle—it is the first mirror of the soul.
Every emotion, every insight, every loss passes through it.
To come home to oneself means to come home to the body.

Stretch.  Walk.  Breathe with attention.
Not to perfect or display, but to feel.
Alexander Lowen said, "To be grounded is to be connected with
one's body, to feel it alive, to know that the feet touch the
earth."
When we inhabit the body fully, anxiety softens—not because
the world changes, but because we have returned to presence.

## The Practice of Silence

Our age worships noise: constant contact, constant doing.
Silence is its rebellion.
But silence is not emptiness; it is the atmosphere where being ripens.

Begin with five quiet minutes—after waking or before sleep.
Sit, breathe, listen.
You do not have to clear the mind; you only have to stay.
Thoughts pass like birds across a wide sky.
This is the field where the unconscious speaks in its own language.

Over time, silence becomes intimate rather than lonely.
It is not withdrawal but communion.

## Reclaiming Rhythm

Nature moves in cycles—day and night, tide and moon.
The Monster's world is linear and relentless.
Healing requires returning to circular time.
Rhythm restores sanity.

Eat when hungry, rest when tired, walk without a device.
Alternate work and stillness.
In Waldorf education, the day breathes: concentration and movement, silence and song.
Adults need this too.
Without rhythm, even success turns to fatigue.
With rhythm, life becomes art.

## Relationships as Mirrors of Wholeness

Wholeness is not a solitary achievement.

Just as the infant becomes real in the mother's gaze, the adult becomes real through genuine connection.
The challenge is to relate without losing oneself—to see and be seen without merging.

Practice small honesty: *I feel tired. I need rest. I don't know.*
Such words invite intimacy more than perfection.
When relationships become mirrors of truth rather than performance, the self relaxes.
We discover that love is not fusion but the freedom to be real together.

## The Inner Witness

Beyond all outer mirrors grows the inner witness—the quiet awareness that can hold experience with compassion.
Meditation, therapy, journaling, or reflective solitude strengthen this capacity.
The witness says, *Yes, this too belongs.*
Anger, joy, fatigue, tenderness—all part of one sky.
Wholeness is inclusion without chaos.

## The Role of Imagination

Imagination is the bridge between conscious and unconscious life.
It translates instinct into image, image into action.
When you dream, daydream, or create symbolic rituals, imagination is healing you.

Before sleep, ask gently: *What do I need to understand?*
In the morning, note the image or feeling that came.
Do not analyze at once; let it unfold.
Meaning reveals itself in its own time.

## Healing Through Service

Self-realization completes itself in giving.
When we share our aliveness—through kindness, teaching, art, listening—it multiplies.
Service is not sacrifice; it is participation in the larger body of life.
Each act of compassion repairs the web of separation.
Viktor Frankl wrote, "Meaning is found not in happiness but in responsibility to something greater than oneself."

The True Self matures when it becomes porous: taking and giving, breathing in and out.

## A Daily Mirror of Wholeness

Try this brief daily practice:
1. **Ground** — Sit and feel your contact with the earth.
2. **Notice** — Ask, *What is alive in me right now?*
3. **Accept** — Whisper, *You are allowed.*
4. **Imagine** — See your vitality as color, flame, or animal. Greet it.
5. **Bless** — Place a hand on your heart and say, *Thank you for being here.*

It takes two minutes, but repeated daily it reshapes the nervous system toward safety and self-trust.

## The Spiral of Becoming

Wholeness is not a destination but a spiral.
We revisit the same themes—fear, desire, control, acceptance— at deeper levels each time.

Growth does not erase wounds; it transforms their meaning.
Jung said, "I am not what happened to me; I am what I choose to become."
Each act of awareness turns trauma into wisdom, instinct into insight.
Slowly we learn to live not against our nature but with it.

## Reflection for the Reader

Ask yourself:

*What daily rituals keep me connected to myself?*
*Where do I still act from performance rather than presence?*
*Which creative act makes me feel most alive?*
*Who mirrors my wholeness, and whom do I mirror in return?*

Write without judgment.
Healing is not a project but a friendship—with life, with the world, with your own being.

## Closing

To live consciously in the presence of life—this is wholeness.
Every breath, gesture, and relationship becomes part of one creative movement: the conversation between the human and the divine within.
We no longer chase perfection; we practice participation.
We no longer worship stillness; we dance with rhythm.
We no longer flee the Beast; we walk beside it, both of us looking out upon the world and whispering:
*All of this is me.*

## Chapter Seven

### The Mirror and the Kingdom: Wholeness as Everyday Practice

When a human being becomes whole, the world itself changes texture.
Light seems softer, breath deeper, and time less urgent.
Nothing outside may have shifted, yet everything feels touched by meaning.
It is as if the mirror of the soul has been cleaned, and life finally recognizes itself within us.

The work of healing the first wound—of reconciling Beast and Monster—was never only personal.
Each individual who restores aliveness participates in something larger: the slow re-enchantment of the world.
Wholeness is contagious; it spreads through presence, through kindness, through art.

### The Inner Kingdom

In myth, the healed hero always returns to the kingdom—not as the person who left, but as one who can now rule wisely.
The kingdom represents consciousness itself, the organized life of the psyche.
When instinct, emotion, and thought are no longer at war, the inner realm becomes fertile again.

This kingdom is ruled not by force but by **relationship.**
The true sovereign listens to every voice within—the child, the sage, the lover, the shadow—and lets them converse.
Governance becomes dialogue.
The Beast stands beside the throne, no longer chained but honored as guardian of vitality.

To live this way is to embody what Jung called the *Self*—the organizing principle that harmonizes opposites.
It is not domination, but participation.

## The Mirror Restored

Throughout our journey, the mirror has appeared again and again: the mother's gaze, the fairy tale, the therapist's empathy, the self's reflection.
Each mirror deepens vision.

At first, we needed others to see us.
Later, we learned to mirror ourselves.
Finally, the mirror expands until it includes the whole world.

The mystics have always described this moment.
Meister Eckhart said, "The eye with which I see God is the eye with which God sees me—it is one eye, one seeing, one knowing."
Rumi wrote, "The soul is a mirror, clear and shining. Look in it and see all worlds within."

When perception itself becomes mirror, separation dissolves.
The world ceases to be an object to master and becomes a partner to meet.

## From Insight to Embodiment

Understanding is only half of transformation; embodiment completes it.
Each ordinary act becomes a chance to practice wholeness: the way we listen, cook, speak, breathe, and rest.

To live this way means:
- **Speak truth gently,** without the need to dominate.
- **Move with rhythm,** alternating effort and stillness.
- **Choose curiosity** instead of control when fear arises.
- **Create beauty,** even in small ways.
- **Listen to the body's wisdom** rather than overriding it.
- **Meet others' Beasts** with the same respect you offer your own.

These are not moral rules but invitations to harmony.
Each gesture becomes a brushstroke in the painting of an integrated life.

## Wholeness in Relationship

True relationship begins when two people meet as mirrors of consciousness.
No one needs to be savior or villain.
The question shifts from "Who is right?" to "What is real between us?"
Conflict becomes teacher, not threat.

Such relationships—friendship, love, community—create sacred spaces where the energy of life circulates freely.
Empathy replaces projection; presence replaces performance.

The same energy that once built masks now builds bridges.

Collective healing begins not in systems, but in these quiet moments of authentic contact.

## Society as Mirror

Culture mirrors our collective psyche.
When individuals live divided—true selves hidden behind images—society becomes mechanical, restless, exploitative.
When individuals live connected to their vitality, culture becomes humane.

Every social reform begins as inner reform.
The way we treat children, nature, and one another reflects how we treat the life inside us.
If we fear the Beast, we build systems of control; if we befriend it, we build systems of creativity.

Alice Miller envisioned a future where no child must repress truth to be loved.
Such a world will not come through revolutions of power but through revolutions of presence—teachers, parents, and leaders who dare to feel.
A pedagogy of aliveness could become the foundation of civilization.

## The Spiritual Dimension of Wholeness

Spirituality, in essence, is remembering that we are part of something vast.
But we reach that vastness not by fleeing humanity, but by entering it deeply.

Every authentic spiritual path descends before it ascends—into the body, the heart, the shadow—before rising into light.

When instinct and consciousness unite, divinity becomes experiential.
Ordinary life turns sacramental: bread, water, breath, touch.
Prayer becomes perception itself.

Rudolf Steiner described this as the **etheric Christ**—the living presence of spirit in the world, perceivable only through love. To see it, one must awaken wonder, the mirror of the soul polished of cynicism.

## The New Myth

Our age is hungry for a new story—not one of domination or redemption, but of participation.
*Beauty and the Beast* hinted at it; now we must live its next chapter: the two living together, creating a kingdom where forest and castle belong to the same world.

In this new myth, Saint George does not kill the dragon; he learns its language.
The sword becomes discernment; the armor becomes awareness.
Together they guard the gates of consciousness, ensuring that neither instinct nor intellect rules alone.

This is the image of a new culture: integration instead of conquest, dialogue instead of destruction.

## Everyday Practices for the Kingdom

To bring this vision into daily life, practice small constancies:

1. **Morning grounding** – Before the day begins, feel your breath and body, whisper *I am here.*
2. **Mindful interaction** – When speaking, sense both your tone and the other's response; adjust toward presence.
3. **Evening reflection** – Ask, *Where did I act from fear? Where did I act from truth?*
4. **Weekly creativity** – Create for joy, not outcome.
5. **Regular silence** – Let stillness punctuate your days like rests in music.
6. **Acts of service** – Each day, do one thing that benefits someone or something beyond yourself.

These practices are not perfectionism; they are maintenance of soul.

Living as Mirror

As integration deepens, we become mirrors for others without trying.
Our calm invites calm; our authenticity invites authenticity.
Transformation rarely happens through words alone—it spreads through presence.
Therapists, parents, artists, lovers—all heal most deeply by simply *being real.*

Wholeness radiates quietly.
It needs no advertisement.

The Kingdom Within and Without

Ultimately, the "kingdom" is not elsewhere.
It is the world perceived through integrated eyes.
When the mirror of awareness is clean, heaven and earth meet in every moment.

The Beast looks through our eyes and sees not danger but beauty.
The mind looks through the heart and sees not chaos but rhythm.
The world mirrors back what we have become.

This is the marriage of heaven and earth: instinct made conscious, spirit made embodied, human made whole.

## Reflection for the Reader

*What does wholeness feel like—not as an idea, but as an experience?*
*Where in my life can I act as a mirror for others' aliveness?*
*What old story am I ready to rewrite?*

Let your answers be small seeds.
The kingdom begins wherever awareness meets compassion.

## Closing

We began with separation and the first wound.
We walked through the Beast's awakening, the Monster's disguise, the mirror's return, the dragon's fire, and the pedagogy of aliveness.
Now we arrive not at an ending but at an opening.

Wholeness is not perfection; it is friendship with imperfection.
It is knowing that every fragment belongs, that light includes shadow, that the kingdom of consciousness is built from both suffering and joy.

Every gesture of awareness repairs a piece of the human fabric.

Every act of kindness heals something ancient.
Every moment of presence polishes the mirror through which existence sees itself.

In the end, the Beast, the Mirror, and the Kingdom were never separate.
They are one living reality calling us home—to the place where life and consciousness meet and recognize each other as one.

## PRACTICES OF WHOLENESS
### Living With the Beast

The work of wholeness does not end with understanding.

Insight opens the door, but practice teaches us how to live inside the room.

What follows is not a program, nor a set of techniques to master. These practices are invitations — ways of staying in relationship with what is alive within you.

Move through them slowly. Return to those that speak to you. Leave the rest.

Wholeness grows not through effort, but through contact.

# Working With the Beast in Therapy

Therapy begins when the Beast is finally allowed to enter the room. It often arrives disguised, while the Monster speaks first.

Healing begins not when symptoms disappear, but when experience becomes speakable.

# Dreams, Symbols, and the Language of the Unconscious

The unconscious speaks in images rather than arguments.

Dreams aim at balance, not comfort. The Beast trusts patience.

Creative Rituals for Integration
Creativity gives form to what cannot yet be spoken.

Honesty, not beauty, heals.

# Love, Projection, and the Inner Mirror

Love awakens early patterns of longing and fear.

Healing comes when we reclaim our projections.

# Guided Reflections & Practices

Meeting the Beast — What part of me still waits for permission to live?

The First Wound — What did I learn about love through separation?

The False Self — Where do I perform instead of feel?

The Monster's Gift — How did adaptation once protect me?

Dream Images — What symbols return repeatedly in my inner life?

The Body Speaks — Where do I feel truth before I understand it?

Creative Fire — Which form of expression restores my vitality?

Love as Mirror — What do I seek in others that belongs to me?

Anger and Boundaries — What wants protection in me?

Integration — What would wholeness look like today?

ॐ

## Epilogue

### The Gaze That Remains

There comes a moment, after long work—analysis, reflection, or creation—when words grow still.
The story has been told, yet something inside continues to listen.
It is no longer waiting for understanding.
It is waiting for *contact*.

Perhaps all healing ends here: not in perfection or knowledge, but in presence—
a gaze that meets the gaze of life and does not turn away.

When I began this book, I wanted to understand how separation shapes us—
why we build masks, why we fear our own vitality,
why love feels both necessary and dangerous.
But beneath all those questions I found the same quiet truth:
we long to be seen without condition.

To be mirrored not as good or bad, useful or broken, but as living.
When that happens, even for a moment, something ancient exhales inside us.
The Beast lies down.
The mirror clears.
The kingdom becomes one landscape—inner and outer, no longer divided.

Each of us carries this possibility.
We do not have to invent it; we only have to remember it.
It appears whenever we look with kindness—
into another's eyes, into the sky, into ourselves.

If this book leaves you with anything, let it be permission:
to feel deeply,
to imagine freely,
to rest without guilt,
to love without armor.

Let the Beast walk beside you as a companion, not a secret.
Let the Monster rest; thank it for its service.
Let the mirror of your awareness reflect the world with tenderness,
knowing that whatever you see is part of yourself.

Wholeness is not a state we reach but a way we look.
The work continues wherever there is a gaze that can remain.

— *Giorgi Khatiashvili*

# Acknowledgments

No book is born in isolation, especially a book about connection.
Every page here carries the echoes of conversations, silences,
and shared discoveries that have shaped my life and work.

My deepest gratitude goes to my teachers, supervisors, and
colleagues who helped me learn how to listen—to others and to
myself.
Your questions were often harder than your answers, and that
was the true teaching.

To my patients, whose courage to explore their inner worlds
made this work possible: thank you.
You have shown me, again and again, that healing is not a
method but a relationship.

I also thank the thinkers whose ideas guided my path:
Donald Winnicott, Otto Rank, Alice Miller, Rudolf Steiner, Bruno
Bettelheim, Marie-Louise von Franz, Carl Jung, Wilfred Bion,
Alexander Lowen, Daniel Stern, Viktor Frankl, and Rainer Maria
Rilke—
each of whom gave language to what the soul already knew.

To my friends and fellow travelers who encouraged me through
years of study, writing, and doubt—your faith reminded me that
creation, too, needs mirroring.

And to those dearest to my heart, who held space for both my
silence and my fire:

your presence lives in every line.

May this book be my way of giving back—a reflection of the light you helped me find.

— *Giorgi Khatiashvili*

# References

Anzieu, D. (1989). *The Skin-Ego.* Yale University Press.

Bettelheim, B. (1976). *The Uses of Enchantment: The Meaning and Importance of Fairy Tales.* Knopf.

Bion, W. R. (1962). *Learning from Experience.* Heinemann.

Bly, R. (1990). *Iron John: A Book about Men.* Addison-Wesley.

Bowlby, J. (1969). *Attachment and Loss, Vol. 1: Attachment.* Basic Books.

Dweck, C. S. (2006). *Mindset: The New Psychology of Success.* Random House.

Frankl, V. E. (1959). *Man's Search for Meaning.* Beacon Press.

Jung, C. G. (1956). *Symbols of Transformation.* Princeton University Press.

Jung, C. G. (2009). *The Red Book (Liber Novus).* W. W. Norton & Company.

Kalsched, D. (1996). *The Inner World of Trauma: Archetypal Defenses of the Personal Spirit.* Routledge.

Lowen, A. (1958). *The Language of the Body.* Macmillan.

Miller, A. (1980). *The Drama of the Gifted Child: The Search for the True Self.* Basic Books.

Rank, O. (1999). *The Trauma of Birth.* Dover Publications.

Rilke, R. M. (2004). *Letters to a Young Poet* (M. Mitchell, Trans.). Modern Library.

Steiner, R. (1995). *The Education of the Child: And Early Lectures on Education.* Anthroposophic Press.

Stern, D. N. (1985). *The Interpersonal World of the Infant.* Basic Books.

Von Franz, M. L. (1970). *The Interpretation of Fairy Tales.* Spring Publications.

Winnicott, D. W. (1960). *The Maturational Processes and the Facilitating Environment.* International Universities Press.

Winnicott, D. W. (1965). *The Family and Individual Development.* Tavistock.

## About the Author

**Giorgi Khatiashvili** is a psychoanalyst, writer, and artist whose work bridges psychology, art, and spiritual science.
Trained in modern psychoanalysis, his practice and research explore how early wounds can transform into creative and spiritual growth.

Born in Tbilisi, Georgia, and educated internationally, Khatiashvili unites Western depth psychology with Eastern contemplative traditions and the symbolic language of myth. His writing speaks equally to clinicians, artists, and seekers, combining analytic precision with poetic sensitivity.

Alongside his clinical and teaching work, he continues to paint, write, and explore the intersection of inner life and culture. *The Beast Within: A Journey from Separation to Wholeness* is his first book—an offering to all who long to live more consciously, courageously, and alive.

## Dedication

**For every friend whose meeting brought transformation—**
those brief encounters and enduring bonds that turned mirrors
into gateways,
and helped me remember who I am.


Art for front cover done by Giorgi Khatiashvili
Author's Portrait used for back cover done by an Artist Iva
Kimeridze

Made in the USA
Middletown, DE
31 January 2026

27489061R00050